How Bear Lost his Tail

Retold by Lucy Bowman
Illustrated by Ciaran Duffy

Reading consultant:
University of Roehampton

Once upon a time, Bear
had a long, thick tail.

The other animals
loved his tail.

Bear didn't like it at all.

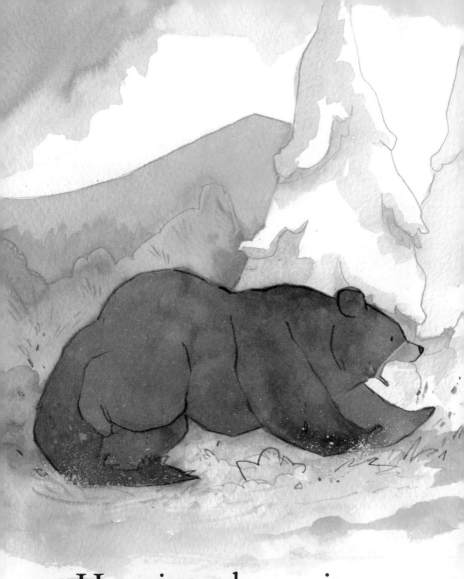

He tripped over it
when he was walking.

It tickled his nose
when he tried to sleep.

Atishoo!

Little animals would
even ride on it.

"Bear's tail is better than mine," thought Fox.

8

He decided to play
a trick on him.

9

He crept over to
a fisherman

and took a
few fish.

Fox carried the fish to
an ice hole in the lake.

12

Bear smelled them.
He came closer.

Rumbl
Rumble

"Those fish look
delicious," said Bear.

14

"I can show you how to
catch them," said Fox.

"Put your tail in the
hole," Fox told Bear.

16

"The fish will bite it and you can pull them out."

It may take some time.

Bear waited and waited.

Day became night.

The night grew cold.
It began to snow.

The next day, Fox
came back. Was
Bear still there?

Fox could only see a
huge heap of snow.

"Bear?" he shouted.

Bear jumped up. But his tail had frozen in the lake...

SNAP!

It broke off.

"I'm so sorry!" Fox
cried. "I didn't know
that would happen."

Bear looked at his new
short tail, and smiled.

Bear padded away —
and he didn't trip once.

PUZZLES

Puzzle 1

Choose the best speech bubble for each picture.

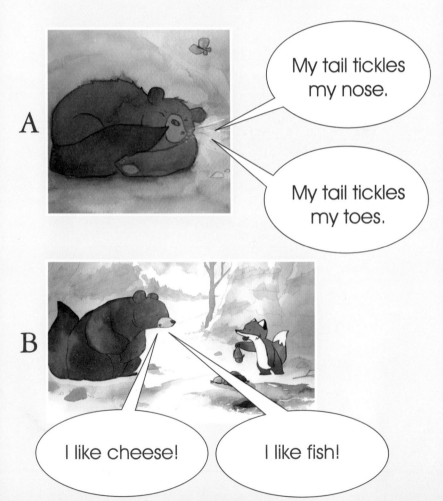

Puzzle 2

Find these things in the picture:

bag   fish   Fox

hat   lake   man

Puzzle 3

Can you spot the differences between these two pictures?

There are six to find.

Answers to puzzles

Puzzle 1

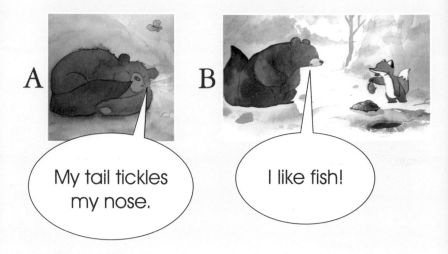

A

My tail tickles my nose.

B

I like fish!

Puzzle 2

hat

man

bag

Fox

fish

lake

Puzzle 3

About the story

How Bear Lost his Tail is based on
a Native American folk legend. It
has been passed down through the
ages by people telling the story to
their children.

Designed by Caroline Spatz
Series editor: Lesley Sims
Series designer: Russell Punter